To Miriam,
   Who already
knows how to
say all the
"right" things!
   Love,
   Betty
   2-14-99

Heartfelt ways to say...

I Love You

by
Candace Hoover

Sterling Publishing Co. Inc., New York
A Sterling/Chapelle Book

Heartfelt Ways to Say I Love You

Owner: Jo Packham
Art Design: Candace Hoover
Book Design: Laura Best
Editorial: Ginger Mikkelsen

Images © 1996 Photodisc,

Library of Congress Cataloging-in-Progress Data

Heartfelt ways to say I love you / [complied] by Candace Hoover.
      p.   cm.
   "A Sterling/Chapelle book."
    ISBN 0-8069-0819-X
    1. Love--Quotations, maxims, etc.   I. Hoover, Candace.
 BF575.L8H375   1998
    302.3--dc21   97-46980
                                                             CIP

10 9 8 7 6 5 4 3 2 1

A Sterling/Chapelle Book
Published by Sterling Publishing Company, Inc.
387 Park Avenue South, New York, NY 10016
©1998 by Chapelle Ltd.
Distributed in Canada by Sterling Publishing
c/o Canadian Manda Group, One Atlantic Avenue, Suite 105
Toronto, Ontario, Canada M6K 3E7
Distributed in Great Britain and Europe by Cassell PLC
Wellington House, 125 Strand London WCR2 0BB, England
Distributed in Australia by Capricorn Link (Australia) Pty Ltd.
P.O. Box 6651, Baulkham Hills, Business Centre NSW 2153, Australia

Sterling ISBN 0-8069-0819-X

Every effort has be
made to ensure th
of the information
this book is accura

If you have any
questions or comm
please contact:
Chapelle Ltd. Inc.
P.O. Box 9252
Ogden, UT 84409
Phone (801) 621-277.
FAX (801) 621-2788

To Mom,
*whose love has
always been there
for me.*

Anonymous

The rose speaks
of love silently,
in a language
known only to
the heart.

and the *reward*

Jane Smiley

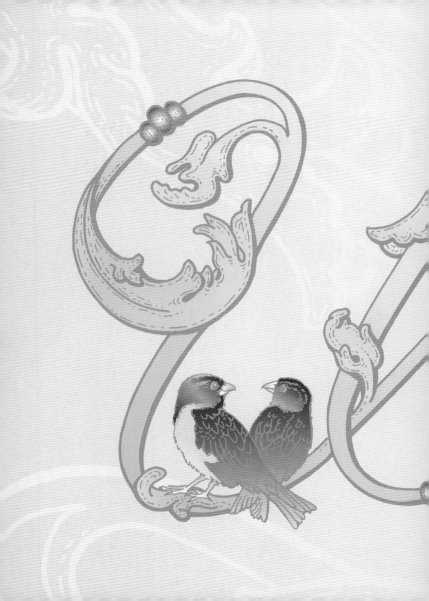

ntil I truly loved,
I was alone.

aroline Sheridan Norton

The world is full of *Beauty* when the heart is full of love.

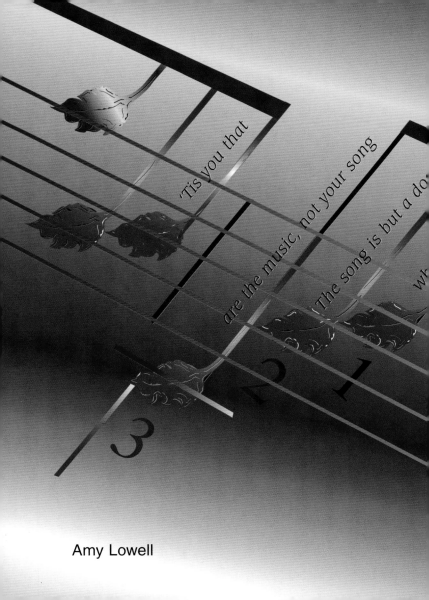

'Tis you that are the music, not your song

The song is but a do...

wh...

Amy Lowell

ng

wide,

lets forth the pent-up

melody inside your

spirit's harmony which,

clear and strong,

sings but of you.

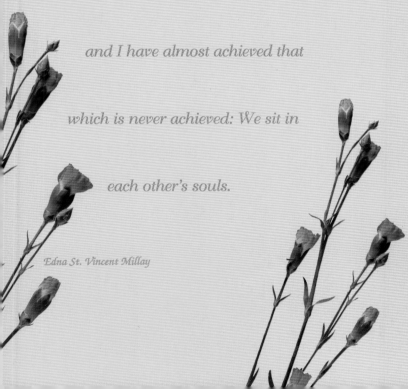

No one can ever take your place

with me. We know each other in

such a certain windless way. You

and I have almost achieved that

which is never achieved: We sit in

each other's souls.

Edna St. Vincent Millay

usic is

love

in search of a word.

Sidney Lanier

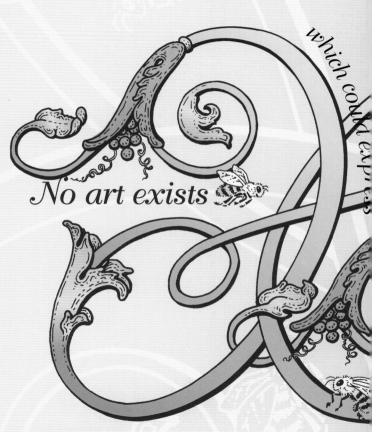

No art exists which could express

Vasilii Zhukovsky

the wonder of

y o u !

Twas not into
my ear you
whispered but
into my heart.

-Judy Garland

There is so much

Friendship

in love, and so

much love in

friendship,

that it would

be futile to ask

where friendship ends

and where love begins.

Elizabeth Selden

People touch our lives, if only for a moment; and yet we're not the same, from that moment on.

The time is not important: the moment is forever.

Fern Bork

We are crazy.

People have sa

Ray Bradbury

But being craz

We know it.

Yet we go on.

together is just fine.

All for you!

Strong and true,
No time the tie can sever,
Till the angels doubt
and the stars burn out,

I am your friend forever.

Samuel Minturn Peck

Thanks for the last time we were together.

*L*ove is everything...

It really is worth fighting for,
being brave for,
risking everything for.
 And the trouble is,
if you don't risk anything,
 you risk even more.

Erica Jong

Love said, "Lie still and think
of me,"
Sleep, "Close your eyes till break
of day,"
But dreams came by and smilingly
Gave both to love and sleep their
way.

Love said, "Lie stil

and think of me,"

Sarah Teasdale

The language of Friendship

is not words

but meanings.

Henry David Thoreau

You may

you may fall from above, but the greatest f

fall fro

you'll ever have is when you fall in

Love

Susan J. Gordon

They came to tell
your faults to me,
They named them
over one by one;

I laughed aloud when
they were done,
I knew them all so
well before -
Oh, they were blind,
too blind to see.
Your faults had made
me love you more.

Sara Teasdale

*H*ow many times we must have met
    Children of chance we were, who passed
Here on the street as strangers a
    The door of heaven and never knew.

Sarah Teasdale

In well-cool hollow walk your way

In bee-soft bower sleep you

in dream, in hom

In drift, in dream, drink fresh,

breathe free; in dream

in home, love keep yo

Mary Phelp

love keep you

I am conscious only of doing
the thing that I love to do -
that I have to do -
and I have to be your friend.

Edna St. Vincent Millay

nd the son

rom beginning to end, I found in the heart of a friend.

Henry Wadsworth Longfellow

h

the miraculous

energy

that flows between two people

who care enough to take the risks

of responding with the whole

heart.

Alex Noble

IT SEEMS TO ME THAT THE COMING OF LOVE IS
LIKE THE COMING OF

pring–

the date is not to be reckoned by the

caelndar. It may be slow and gradual; it may

be quick and sudden. But in the morning,

when we wake and recognize a change in the

world without, blossoms on the sward,

warmth in the sunshine, music in the air, we

say Spring has come.

Edward George Bulwer-Lytton

Kindred

spirits

are rather illusive

Nancy Lindemeyer

I guess we have

to be content with

the notion that   *we will always*

know them when   *we see them.*

The primary condition of friendship is

Joy

the delight of recognizing yourself
in another and finding in them the
person you have, consciously or
unconsciously, always been seeking;
at least you knew them to be there,
waiting for you somewhere, even as
you were waiting for them.

Elizabeth Selden

The face of all the world is changed,

I think since first I heard
the footsteps of thy soul.

- Elizabeth Barrett Browning

Take

Quick

and tell me,

What have yo

my hand

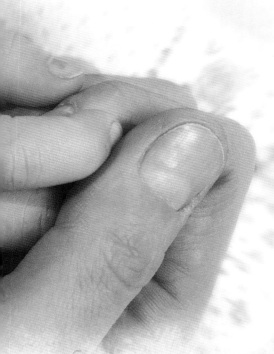

...n your heart.

A. E. Housman

ive

*Love is what
gives today
a future.*

g ve

*Love is what
gives the
winter sprin*

gi e

*It gives my
storms their
rainbow*

giv

*and gives to
my life most
everything.*

Your vision will become clear

only when you can look into your own heart.

Who looks outside, dreams:

*who looks inside, **awakes.***

Carl Jung

I cannot tell the spell that

Annie Chambers-Ketchum

inds

thine image forever
in my heart.
I only know thou
art to my
existence its very
vital part.

To love a person is to learn
the song that is in their heart,

and sing it to them when they have forgotten.

Thomas Chandler

I have not spent a

ay

Napoleon Bonaparte (to Josephine Bonaparte; 1796)

without loving you...

In our life there is a single color,

as on an artist's palette,

which provides the meaning of life and art

Marc Chagall

It is the

olor of

love.

Love is the only flower that grows and blossoms

without the aid of seasons.

Kahlil Gibra

The *zest* of life
is found in *joy*, in
giving, in *sharing*
and *laughter* but
most of all in
love.

I believe that imagination

is stronger than knowledge.

That myth is more potent than history.

I believe that dreams are more powerful than facts.

That hope triumphs over experience.

That laughter is the only cure for grief

and I believe that love is stronger than death.

Robert Fulghum